BAGGAGE CLAIM

Daily Devotional

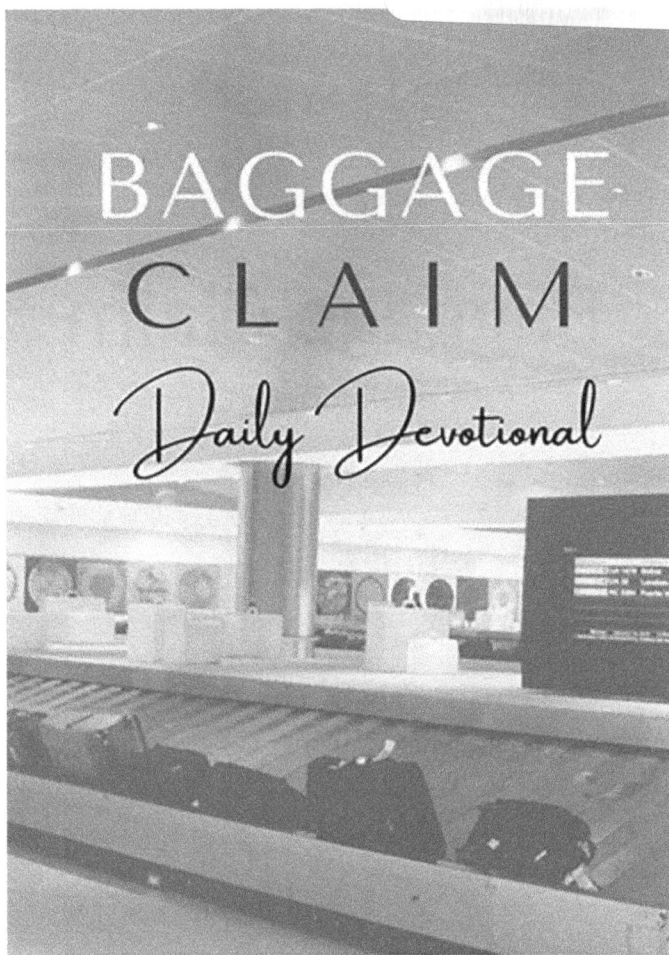

CARL DIXON

Baggage Claim

Carl A. Dixon

ISBN: 978-1-943409-85-3

Printed in the United States of America

In loving memory of my Father Carl E. Dixon

From my first step to your last breath, I have learned that the more life you lose, the more valuable it becomes. Trying to highlight your presence, your strength and your love, is like trying to capture the ocean with a coffee cup. Thank you for giving your all. From that I have aspired not to have more but to be more. Words can never express how much I miss you.

Table of Contents

Acknowledgements

My Mom once told me that an inheritance isn't what you leave to people. But what you leave in people. This book is a team effort, a reflection of what my mother, sister and entire family left in me. They inspired me to listen to God. I have to thank one of the most beautiful and brilliant souls I know Ameerah. One of best parts of my life is you. I am extremely fortunate to have you as my confidant, my companion, my wife. The best is yet to come. I also want to thank Pastor Jerome Barber, who believed in me in ways that I didn't believe in myself. Thank you to the city of Chicago that taught me the meaning of resilience and strength. To Calvary Missionary Baptist Church for loving me and teaching me as a child. Finally, thank you to every friend, confidant, associate, and advisor. You all have shown me that purpose is truly a gift from above.

Preface

Spiritual liberation isn't just a figment of our imagination, it's a tangible reality. Throughout life we find ourselves in what feels like baggage weighing us down, preventing us from moving forward. The very baggage that weighs us down, is the same baggage we are ashamed to claim due to the negative stigma and public humiliation it comes with. What if I told you claiming that baggage was the key to your freedom?

In John 5, Jesus has an encounter with a lame man and ask Him a question God has been asking us ever since we could recognize His voice, "Do you want to be made well?". If we don't allow our pride to subside to our humility when God ask us such questions like these, it's easy to forfeit your freedom. Pride will make you believe that you have nothing to be healed from, no problems, no baggage to claim. Ironically, Jesus asked this rhetorical question not wondering if He wanted healing after dealing with an infliction for thirty-eight years, but seeing if the man would claim his baggage.

His response to Jesus was his way of admitting that he has been carrying the weight of his baggage and desired to be released of it. Embrace your baggage! God is not exposing your baggage to shame you; He is exposing your baggage to dispose of it. The first step to freedom is the confession to

God that, "Yes I have baggage!". Only then can the operation of Holy Spirit fully commence and liberation begin to take place in your life.

This book is designed for you to identify your unique baggage. Your baggage is nothing to be ashamed of, we all have baggage! The true question is how long will you ignore the baggage weighing you down that Jesus ultimately desires to release from your life?

-Marquis Cotton.

2020

Joshua 5:11-12
Joshua 6:2-3

"The very next day they began to eat unleavened bread and roasted grain harvested from the land. No manna appeared on the day they first ate from the crops of the land, and it was never seen again. So, from that time not the Israelites ate from the crops of Canaan"- Joshua 5: 11-12 NLT

"But the Lord said to Joshua, "I have given you Jericho, its king, and all its strong warriors. You and your fighting men should march around the town once a day for six days." - Joshua 6:2-3 NLT

In order for God to do something NEW, Eating from the promise land (Joshua 5:11). He must stop what we know to be normal (manna Joshua 5:12). He's creating a different appetite in us. A new menu

2020 (appetite) means there is about to be new movements from God (Joshua 6:2-3). It's like God is changing the channel so that what others have talked about (Moses) but never touched can finally be seen and obtained (Jericho).

The Three Ments

———⊂✕⊃———

Joshua 5:8-

"**A**nd after the whole nation had been circumcised, they remained where they were in camp until they were healed. Then the Lord said to Joshua, "Today I have rolled away the reproach of Egypt from you."

So, the place has been called Gilgal to this day."-Joshua 5:8-9 NIV

There is a difference in being delivered from a place (Egypt) and being delivered within yourself. Three things in life are MENT. 1. To be delivered from self, to the total reliance on God (developMENT). 2. To cut away fleshly attitudes (improveMENT) 3. To be Spirit led (moveMENT). The same place where you are feeling the most pain, is the same place where you will receive the most healing from God. The reason why most of us struggle with healing is because healing requires, we do two things. 1) Sitting still 2) Exposure. We don't like sitting still and being exposed. When God puts you in a position to heal, he will put people around you that will not interrupt or be intimidated by what you are healing from. If you're healing, you're not hiding. If you're hiding, you're not healing! The reason why certain relationships from your past died off (in the wilderness) was because you can hurt with everybody, but you can't heal with just anybody. Healing removes shame. The healing hand of God removes/rolls away (Gilgal) what was blocking our commitment to his plan/promises for our future. For forty years the Israelites wander in the wilderness in circles. Here in Joshua 5, they are finally in line with God's vision for their life. Lack of direction not lack of time is the problem that we all have. The Wilderness took 14,600 days and the Walls of Jericho took 7 days. When you are in that place that you are purposed to be in, you will accomplish more than ever before in a shorter period of time. Allow God to lead you to what He promised, even if it means abandoning the lifestyles and relationships that are attached to the wilderness. Become more focused on where God is taking you, instead of who's not coming with you.

(A Gift for Jaylen)

Overlooked

———◦∞◦———

1 Samuel 16:10-12

"In the same way all seven of Jesse's sons were presented to Samuel. But Samuel said to Jesse, "The LORD has not chosen any of these." Then Samuel asked, "Are these all the sons you have?" "There is still the youngest," Jesse replied. "But he's out in the fields watching the sheep and goats." "Send for him at once," Samuel said. "We will not sit down to eat until he arrives." So, Jesse sent for him. He was dark and handsome, with beautiful eyes. And the LORD said,

"This is the one; anoint him".

When Samuel showed up to anoint the next king for God, David's father recommended all of his brothers except David. Being overlooked by someone you love can create an overwhelming feeling of doubt and despair. David's father was making an invalid attempt to ostracize him from God's plan. Unfortunately, there will be times when family and loved ones will believe that promotion and progress should be given to everyone except you. The beautiful thing about God is that he doesn't require anybody's opinion on His plan for your destiny. Just because you're not visible to people, doesn't mean you don't have value in God's eyes. What we must learn here is that Samuel was able to acknowledge and celebrate what God was doing because he listened to God (the name Samuel means God has heard).

Someone that doesn't hear from God will never see or understand what God is about to do with their life. David was the eighth child and eight symbolizes a new beginning. New beginnings usually guarantee purpose, promotion and power (David was about to be King). With God your destiny is tailor made; it won't fit anybody but you. In order to begin new, you have to respond to God's promise and acceptance not the rejection of people.

Hide and Seek

Exodus 2:12-17

"After looking in all directions to make sure no one was watching, Moses killed the Egyptian and hid the body in the sand. The next day, when Moses went out to visit his people again, he saw two Hebrew men fighting. "Why are you beating up your friend?" Moses said to the one who had started the fight. The man replied, "Who appointed you to be our prince and judge? Are you going to kill me as you killed that Egyptian yesterday?" Then Moses was afraid, thinking,

"Everyone knows what I did." And sure enough, Pharaoh heard what had happened, and he tried to kill Moses. But Moses fled from Pharaoh and went to live in the land of Midian. When Moses arrived in Midian, he sat down beside a well. Now the priest of Midian had seven daughters who came as usual to draw water and fill the water troughs for their father's flocks. But some other shepherds came and chased them away. So, Moses jumped up and rescued the girls from the shepherds. Then he drew water for their flocks."

Ever since I was a little boy, my father would tell me that failure is a result, not a person. He was helping me to understand that failure isn't fatal—it's normal! So, in other words, failure is a bruise, not a tattoo. I have failed collegiate exams. I have failed family and friends who were relying on me. I have failed to always speak the truth. I have failed to deliver at work. I know that there are people reading this who feel their failures are much bigger or harder to come back from. Just look around; we all make mistakes from time to time and sometimes more than we would like to admit.

Unfortunately, we tend to overly focus on our own shortcomings, and that robs us of our confidence to succeed. This was the premise for one of the greatest spiritual leaders found in scripture, Moses. Scripture says that Moses killed a man and buried him in the sand. The next day he made an attempt to break up a fight between two Hebrew men and someone mentioned his mistake. Being confronted by something that he thought he hid, it caused him to run.

Many of us are running in life because of what we have been hiding. From this unhealthy outlook, we find ourselves running from people, our purpose, and our problems. Like Moses, we think hiding our mistakes erases them, but it doesn't. We have to stop thinking survival is success. Moses had survived his mistake, but he wasn't successful at this point in his life. I believe we have survived much, but we are not at the place of success that God intended. The Bible says after Moses ran, he took up residence in Midian and was sitting beside a well. Then seven daughters of a Midian priest came to draw water and take care of their father's flock. Suddenly a shepherd came and chased the young ladies away. Moses then jumped up and rescued the young ladies from the shepherds and drew water for their flocks. Here we see that he did things differently than before. Like Moses, we have two choices when it comes to our mistakes: *Either we live in them or we learn from them.*

Either you will be a travel agent or a tour guide. This means you will either talk about movement while remaining complacent or you will use your experience and wisdom to create movement inside yourself and others that will help them find places in life they never knew existed. When our motives honor ourselves, we hurt people. When our motives honor God, we help people. When we change our motives in life, it changes our motions.

Healthy Worship

—⌛—

1 Kings 18:30-40

"Then Elijah called to the people, "Come over here!" They all crowded around him as he repaired the altar of the Lord that had been torn down. He took twelve stones, one to represent each of the tribes of Israel, and he used the stones to rebuild the altar in the name of the Lord. Then he dug a trench around the altar large enough to hold about three gallons. He piled wood on the altar, cut the bull into pieces, and laid the pieces on the wood. Then he said, "Fill four large jars with water, and pour the water over the offering and the wood." After they had done this, he said, "Do the same thing again!" And when they were finished, he said, "Now do it a third time!" So, they did as he said, and the water ran around the altar and even filled the trench. At the usual time for offering the evening sacrifice, Elijah the prophet walked up to the altar and prayed, "O Lord, God of Abraham, Isaac, and Jacob, prove today that you are God in Israel and that I am your servant. Prove that I have done all this at your command. O Lord answer me! Answer me so these people will know that you, O Lord, are God and that you have brought them back to yourself." Immediately the fire of the Lord flashed down from heaven and burned up the young bull, the wood, the stones, and the dust. It even licked up all the water in the trench! And when all the people saw it, they fell face down on the ground and cried out, "The Lord —he is God! Yes, the Lord is God!" Then Elijah commanded, "Seize all the prophets of Baal. Don't let a single one escape!" So, the people seized them all, and Elijah took them down to the Kishon Valley and killed them there."

1 Kings 18:30-40 NLT

When you are in God's vineyard: Mount Caramel (sphere of consistent activity), there will be opposition with people that you will be familiar with. It's in this atmosphere you are made aware of what people including yourself are submitted to. Whether it be the eternal God or the artificial imitation Baal. With God the creator, he wishes to restore and liberate the soul. Baal means owner, Satan (he's a slumlord). He likes making people pay a price for a place in their life that he doesn't own.

There is a difference in living around the altar and living on the altar. The prophets of Baal shouted and danced but it wasn't to honor God. It was to honor what owned them. They were simply just living around a broken altar. When we worship anything outside of God, our intimacy (altar) stays in a state of brokenness. If our intimacy with God is broken, so is our intimacy with others. Elijah's name means Jehovah is God. Only God can restore our intimacy with Him. We simply have to deny being owned by the world, our worries, our money and our mistakes. Submit our heart and hands to God and he will rebuild in us (new heart) and through us. He does this so we can live on the altar (living sacrifice) and arrest what disturbs our commitment to Him.

Now here's where God messed me up. He says you have watched me move and watched my power fall into your situation. However, you never arrested what I gave you authority over. When God gives us authority through His spirit (Brook Kishon) it's to dismember the devices and curses of the enemy. But He said Carl, you usually negotiate with what was harming you and our relationship. Meaning I pray, God moves, and I say a few words. But I allow the device to escape. He said son during negotiations a person can always leave. In order to be free, you have to stop negotiating with something I called you to crush!!

Overworked and Underpaid

---∞---

Luke 5:3-60

T hen he got into one of the boats, which was Simon's, and asked him to put out a little from the land. He then sat down and taught the multitudes from the boat. When he had stopped speaking, He said to Simon, "Launch out into the deep and let down your nets for a catch." But Simon answered and said to Him, "Master, we have toiled all night and caught nothing; nevertheless, at your word, I will let down the net." And when they had done this, they caught a great number of fish, and their net was breaking."

Luke 5:3-6 NKJV

Have you ever felt like you were at a space in life where you were finished with the same routines, same relationships, or same problems? Don't worry, you're not alone I have felt the same way. I heard a

Pastor say something profound. *Just because you're finished, doesn't mean God says you're done.* He was speaking from the context of Luke 5:6-7. In that scripture, we have the Master interacting with our favorite disciple Peter. Here's what I learned from that.

- When hope collides with hopelessness, it creates a fresh start and Christ will step into your problem (boat).

- When he steps in, he takes you to places that you have overlooked due to rejection, tiredness, or emptiness.

- God pushes us past our failures, and he tells him to push out into the deep.

- God steps into your problem and begins to teach us /others through our problem.

- God then redefines and redirects the use of everything in your life that is connected to your hands and heart.

He then told Peter to use the same net that previously made him feel empty. Failures make us start giving up on the right things (the net, love, forgiveness, trust, marriage) that we need for growth. The net represents faith. Sometimes we are in the right place but position our faith in the wrong things, so we often times come up empty.

God turns our hurt into healing while we are still in a position to face the same things that have hurt us and while the pain is fresh. Peter was still in the place that he failed in.

Before we heal, we must be willing to push past our hurt and tiredness and respond to God's word. We must not put our faith back into the net or our own thoughts, but into God's word. The word with the spirit (water) of God equals new results and an abundance beyond measure (the net broke). It causes such an abundance that we must worship and confess that the problem was never with the net, the situation or the people around us, but with ourselves. Through obedience and integrity God opens a new door. A door of Destiny. God uses the emptiness to get your attention that he's about to fill what you have missed. God can take us past our failures. If

I'm still stuck, it's safe to say it's because of me. My question is what are you stuck on?

----

[1] *Huge thank you to Sheena, Homer, Rodney, Marquis, Deric, Q, Jacob, Brian Darden, James Ransome, Barocka Pankins and many others that have helped me on the days when my net was empty.*

Shining Star

Esther 4:15-16

"Then Esther sent this reply to Mordecai: "Go and gather together all the Jews of Susa and fast for me. Do not eat or drink for three days, night or day. My maids and I will do the same. And then, though it is against the law, I will go in to see the king. If I must die, I must die.""

Esther 4:15-16 NLT

A witness (Esther means star) (She was a light in a dark place).

Esther was a witness for the Kingdom. A witness is what you are and it's far more than something that you do. A witness gathers others and establishes the value of following Christ. You will never find your purpose if you are trapped by your preferences. When it comes to nurturing and strengthening your thought process (Romans 12:2), your focus is your fuel. Your focus must be scriptural not situational.[1] Esther was willing to do something that went against the social norm.

She understood in order to invoke healthy change that honors God, she could not conform.

Elevators are necessary inside of a structure. Elevators allow you to reach places quicker than you would on your own.

Only the light of God can elevate and reveal something new.

That light resides in us (2 Cor 4:7). We are all lights (Matt 5:14-16). If nobody gathers around you and can see/hear

God better, you're not a light/star (Esther) you're a noise

(Haman)

If you're not willing to lose for God, you're not really fighting to win.

God uses circumstances/systems as catapults to put His servants into a place they could not reach on their own.

Esther was an elevator and innovator.

Women pursuing their purpose from God bring others up and introduce something that's never been seen by anyone except God.

(A Gift to Alaina)

Faces

Ezekiel 1:10

"As for the likeness of their faces, each had the face of a man; each of the four had the face of a lion on the right side, each of the four had the face of an ox on the left side, and each of the four had the face of an eagle."

Ezekiel 1:10 NKJV

Now that you know these things, you will be blessed if you do them. Jesus was our example of a SERVANT. He was our example of SACRIFICE. If we are truly the SPIRITUALLY renewed people that God has called us to be, we will have the face of an OX, the face of sacrifice. The 2nd face that Ezekiel's vision speaks of is THE FACE OF A MAN. This face represents RELATIONSHIP, and again, we find the perfect example in Jesus. Jesus did not live a solitary life. He was part of an earthly

FAMILY with extended family ties. He lived in a COMMUNITY with Jewish friends and neighbors. When he began public ministry, he chose to share it in a RELATIONSHIP with 12 handpicked men. With these 12, he shared his life, his ministry and his suffering.

This life of service to the Lord is meant to be shared in every RELATIONSHIP that you have – in the family, in the community, on the job, in public. In every relationship you have, you are called to share your relationship with Christ. The SPIRIT-RENEWED life will do that. When Saul, who later became the great Apostle Paul was initially blinded by the Lord. When he opened his eyes as a Christian, the first thing he saw was the FACE OF A MAN --- Ananias was his name. That special relationship that Saul had with Ananias was powerful. Ananias was used to bring healing to Saul, to baptize him, and to lead him to the fullness of the Holy Spirit. You and I need RELATIONSHIPS. The face of a man shows us our need for valuable, life-affirming relationships.

If we are the Spiritual people that God has called us to be…. if our lives are going to represent the GLORY OF GOD, we will constantly be on the look for such relationships.

The third face that Ezekiel saw was THE FACE OF AN EAGLE. The EAGLE represents TRAINING/DISCIPLESHIP as you increase in Christian maturity and godliness. Psalms 103:5 says, "who satisfies your desires with good things so that your youth is renewed like the eagle's". The Psalmist used this language because the Eagle's life speaks much about the learning process, the process of discipleship. Eagles carefully and methodically train their young to SOAR, to FLY, and to HUNT. They watch over them as they mature, encircling them, caring for them, and guarding them as the apple of their eye. We all need the EAGLES in our lives as Christians. We need those individuals who can MENTOR us, TRAIN us, and

DEVELOP us into all that God has called us to be. If you and I are to live the lives that glorify God, one of the faces that we will have is the face of an EAGLE. Eagles are aware that it's the wind currents that bring them to the higher places. That is what we need to know as DISCIPLES of the Lord. The "winds of adversity" are opportunities to grow stronger in the Lord…to SOAR HIGHER in the things of God. Our lives will represent the glory of God when we grow and mature to the place where we have the FACE OF AN EAGLE to assist the younger in maturity and development in the things of God.

The fourth and final face that Ezekiel saw in his vision was THE FACE OF A LION. This is the glorious face of a child of God, the face of a lion. This face represents our position as an OVERCOMER. It is the culmination of all the other faces. First, we live SACRIFICIAL LIVES. Second, we build RELATIONSHIPS and share that life of servanthood. Third, we grow, mature and help others in discipleship.

Then we reach the culmination of all in life --- we OVERCOME, and we CONQUER the plans that the devil had for our lives. We started ours in COMPASSION and ended up with CONQUEST! The enemy tried to stop us! He pulled out his greatest weapon to use against us – the weapon of FEAR. However, FAITH kills FEAR and Paul reminds us that 2 Timothy 1:7…*For God did not give us a spirit of timidity (FEAR), but a spirit of power, of love and of self-discipline*. Once we have that assurance…that

spirit of power… the Bible says in Proverbs 28:1…
that "the righteous are as bold as a lion." Lions hunt
in packs. They work in conjunction with other lions
in order to surround their enemies and cut off their
escape. They exemplify a TEAM EFFORT and this
way they succeed where if they were ALONE, they
could possibly FAIL. That's what Jesus did. He
formed excellent, disciple teams to go into cities and
shake them up for the Kingdom of God. He gave
them specific instructions. Look at Luke 10:1-3….
*10:1 After this the Lord appointed seventy-two others
and sent them two by two ahead of him to every town
and place where he was about to go. 10:2 He told
them, "The harvest is plentiful, but the workers are
few. Ask the Lord of the harvest, therefore, to send
out workers into his harvest field. 10:3 Go! I am
sending you out like lambs among wolves.* In fact, the
Bible says that God continued to send them out. Acts
17:6 says…." these men turned the world upside
down". That's what God has called you and I to do.
We have the face of an OX – the face of
SACRIFICE. We have the face of a MAN – the face
of RELATIONSHIPS. We have the face of an
EAGLE – the face of TRAINING/MATURITY. We
have the face of a LION – we serve together and
experience VICTORY. That's the face of a

SPIRITUAL MAN/WOMAN. That's the face of a believer who is manifesting the GLORY OF GOD in their life. That's the face that God wants to see on every one of us. It's the face that Ezekiel saw. It's the face that Daniel saw and it's the face that John saw in REVELATION. Sir….

Do you have the face of a SPIRITUAL MAN? Ma'am…Do you have the face of a woman who manifests the glory of God? What about you young person? Do you have the hunger and desire to see your life bring glory to the Lord?

The glory of God brings a spiritual response. Let's let our lives cause others to see the glory of the Lord.

Comfort Kills!

—⟨∞⟩—

Matthew 12:43-45

Written by the prophetic Marquis Cotton.

"When an evil spirit leaves a person, it goes into the desert, seeking rest but finding none. Then it says, 'I will return to the person I came from.' So, it returns and finds its former home empty, swept, and in order. Then the spirit finds seven other spirits eviler than itself, and they all enter the person and live there. And so that person is worse off than before.

That will be the experience of this evil generation."

Matthew 12:43-45 NLT

Never get comfortable to the point of letting your guard down. Satan is waiting for an opportunity to return back to you and to get you back into old habits. But this time it will be a stronger stronghold than before. Satan cannot rest while you are delivered! He is LIKE a lion waiting to devour you! He cannot rest to the point where he gets backup just to ensure your bondage is infinite and generation impacting!

Do not get comfortable…Satan is scheming on you I promise! Stay woke! Keep praying. Keep fasting. Keep reading your Word! Stay surrounded by God-fearing people! Do not choose carnal activities over Godly interactions! Satan is counting on your comfort to distract you from his scheming.

Blind Spot

John 6:5-7

J esus soon saw a huge crowd of people coming to look for him. Turning to Philip, he asked, "Where can we buy bread to feed all these people?" He was testing Philip, for he already knew what he was going to do. Philip replied, "Even if we worked for months, we wouldn't have enough money to feed them!"

Attention is expensive be careful how you spend it. Emptiness can only end when you are looking for (paying attention to) God not people (v5) The greatest invitations to grow closer to God will usually come while you're empty (the people were hungry v5). Sometimes only God will see what's missing in your life not people or disciples (v5). Sometimes you blame other people for something you want (Phillip mentioned and wanted money. The people wanted God). You don't have a good solution for your emptiness but God does (v6). God will push you towards what you want to push away (v7). Our problem is not in what we lack but what we are looking for...

The Dating Game

Judges 16:19-21

" After putting him to sleep on her lap, she called for someone to shave off the seven braids of his hair, and so began to subdue him. And his strength left him. Then she called, "Samson, the Philistines are upon you!" He awoke from his sleep and thought, "I'll go out as before and shake myself free." But he did not know that the Lord had left him. Then the Philistines seized him, gouged out his eyes and took him down to Gaza. Binding him with bronze shackles, they set him to grinding grain in the prison."- Judges 16:1921 NIV

You lay your head in an ungodly place that you can see but it's attached to the proximity of Satan that you can't see. This is how the enemy brings us down in unhealthy relationships. (Judges 16:19)

You can be strong and gifted but be misplaced with God. You can never be free of a problem you misdiagnose.

Delilah keeps you in a place of *purposeless existence*. Bondage always introduces itself in an attractive form.

Sometimes we are so busy focusing on the wrong person, environment, or mindset (Delilah) that we become unconscious of what's right (he was sleeping). We don't realize God has left until our dysfunctional decision (Delilah) has become our alarm clock. (She called out to him). V20

The more you wait on people to change that don't honor God, the closer you are to losing your vision (v20).

Delilah will always be Delilah. Stop waiting on people to not be who they are so you can win (so you can feel better about it).

How do you know I'm waiting on people? You stay in a place designed to enslave you. (Judges 16:21)

For the record this is what Satan is always after, **your vision**. If Satan takes your vision, He gets to lead you down into darkness (v21). They took him down into Gaza. (v21)

Samson shows us just because we are not hurting doesn't mean we are not hurt. Unresolved pain (failed marriage: Judges 15:1-2; unhealthy relationships: Judges 16:1) turn into self-destructive habits.

Dysfunctional relationships are a gateway drug. They open you up to more nonsense. We are all a compilation of the people, places, and experiences we've been exposed to. *What we tune into, we turn into*. Imagine if we tune into God (Matt 14:26-29) ... We come out of what was restricting us.

Desperation detours Destiny. Every detour has a Delilah.

Turning Point

———⟨∞⟩———

Genesis 32: 22-28

"During the night Jacob got up and took his two wives, and his eleven sons and crossed the Jabbok River with them. After taking them to the other side, he sent over all his possessions. This left Jacob all alone in the camp, and a man came and wrestled with him until the dawn began to break. When the man that he would not win the match, he touched

Jacob's hip and wrenched it out of its socket. Then the man said, "Let me go, for the dawn is breaking!" But Jacob said, "I will not let you go unless you bless me." "What is your name?" the man asked. He replied, "Jacob." "Your name will no longer be Jacob," the man told him. "From now on you will be called Israel because you have fought with God and with men and have won." - Genesis 32:22-28 NLT

Removing distractions designates an area in your life void of all things you are accustomed to having around you…where all things you are familiar with can no longer see you and you can no longer see them. Whatever you walk into is determined by what you are willing to walk out of. What you walk out of will bring you closer to God. What did Jacob walk into? A place of surrender, a place of power, a place of being emptied (Jabbok!). New beginnings are born by being emptied by God. What is God emptying me of? The names of Jacob's two wives give us this answer. Leah (the cow / heifer) Genesis 29:31 = unloved / rejected. Leah represents the area of our life where we feel unwanted (rejection). Where we use actions to "purchase / earn" acceptance (Genesis 29:32). God uses rejected people to reveal His power / presence (Judah in Genesis 29:35). God ALWAYS chooses those who have been rejected to bring Jesus to a generation / to the world. Rachel (mature female sheep). Although she was mature and beautiful, Rachel was empty. Rachel represents the part of our life that is beautiful on the outside but IS NOT fruitful on the inside. Rachel represents frustration. In today's culture, we have become skilled in looking good and being liked by others even when we don't like ourselves. Genesis 30:1 says Rachel envied her sister. "…" give me children or I'll die!'" God uses our frustration to give birth (Joseph in Genesis 30:25) to purpose; a dream that only God can assemble.

Get comfortable with being uncomfortable. Isolation with God launches you into your identity / destiny. Launching requires LEAVING. Most of us want to launch, but we don't want to leave anything to get closer to God. When you allow God to work on your reality, you will no longer be able to hide your brokenness behind bushes and being self-sufficient. Why must I be alone for my reality to change? Because God will not allow you to be dependent on something that will deplete you (career, money, marriage, sex, people, possessions (Genesis 32:22-23) At this place God begins to attack (wrestle) with what has misplaced our life (our flesh). Jacob represents our flesh (self-centered + deceptive). Anyone who listens to their flesh is listening to a liar. God touching his hip (corrected his posture /walk). God changing his name (corrected his problem). Your freedom is hidden behind your decisions. You're not going to get a real identity from God until you choose to expose that dysfunctional (deceitful) side of yourself ("…the man asked him his name. He replied, "Jacob." The last time he had been asked his name, he said, "Esau". The lie we live in front of people, cannot be lived in front of God. Before God, you are not who you were. You cannot capture what you don't focus on. You have to choose: Will you cling to the Word of God & grab hold of your identity or will you cling to the mistakes / unhealthy thinking you used to label your life? There is a Jacob in all of us. God uses our limitations as leverage to reveal His strength. So, we can stop being confined by what we see and begin to see what were created to be. Which is triumphant with God (Israel).

Hunger Pains

Matthew 4:2-3

A fter fasting forty days and forty nights, he was hungry.

The tempter came to him and said, "If you are the Son of God, tell these stones to become bread."

Being hungry isn't wrong, it's how you feed your hunger. The enemy/the world is tempting us daily to fill our hunger in an unhealthy/illegitimate manner. God wants us to pay attention to what we turn to fill us when we are empty (hungry). There is a difference between the devil's menu and God's menu. With God He prepares a table for you, feeds you, and anoints you and your cup overflows (Psalm 23:5). With Satan he puts you and what you love on the menu to be eaten (destroyed). Like Christ, it's our choice what we choose. Eat with our Shepherd or be eaten by a snake!

Side Effects of Success

———◦✕◦———

Judges 1:28-29

W hen the Israelites grew stronger, they forced the Canaanites to work as slaves, but they never did drive them completely out of the land. The tribe of Ephraim failed to drive out the Canaanites living in Gezer, so the Canaanites continued to live there among them."

Just because I have become stronger and learned how to manage a problem, does not mean I have alleviated the problem. To become stronger but nothing changes, means I have based my progress on my pleasure and my profit (slaves) but not my purpose from God.

Do not trade the *ultimate* for the *immediate*. When you do, your problems stay in the same place. The word Ephraim means double fruitful: meaning successful. Success does not remove struggles. One can give the perception of being fruitful but without being faithful to God, the place that God wants you to attack is dividing (Gezer) your attention, your peace, and your progress.

The beginning of God doing something amazing (His promises) is at the end of your efforts to be successful without Him (His word). The Israelites were very much like us. They had experienced a dysfunctional relationship through their oppression with the Egyptians. Dysfunctional relationships are a gateway drug. They make us comfortable recycling things that should be replaced. Even though God brought the Israelites out of Egypt to a new place, they were still comfortable being close to dysfunction (anything that dishonors God and His plan). The Israelites were fighting to revive where they had been, instead of opening their hearts and eyes wider to where they were supposed to be.

Wealth and Worry

———∞———

Matthew 6:19-24

For me the Bible is infallible, and it touches on every circumference of our lives. Here we find God (Christ Jesus) in the flesh discussing wealth and worry. God empowers us with the question, "Where is your treasure?" and helps us find the answer through the concept of four tests. - Matthew 6:19-24

The first test is the DURABILTY TEST and we find it in verses 19-20. Christ instructs us, "do not store up for yourselves treasures on earth, where moth and rust destroy, and where thieves break in and steal." From this we have our first test, "How long will these things last?" Meaning how durable are the possessions that we believe are valuable in our eyes. Why is it that we put more value into possessions and people than our relationship with God? The answer begins with a G and ends with a D but it's not God...

its *greed*. Verse 20, God tells us the only place where we should be storing treasures is in heaven.

The word that jumps out of these texts are "treasures". Notice that Christ did not use the word *money* in these texts. God knows everyone may not have Serena Williams and Jeff Bezos' money, but everyone has something they treasure. God is not saying that it is wrong to have treasures; He is telling us that our focus should be on laying up treasures in heaven, not on earth. Greed coupled with being misguided leads to materialism (i.e. Judas; Luke 12:16-21). God is not forbidding us to own anything, the key lies in the little phrase, "for yourselves he is forbidding us from being self- centered and not Christ-centered.

God is trying to teach us a life skill to stop living just for today also known as the moment or convenience. This command is in the present tense. It literally means to "stop storing up." We're to stop doing something that by nature we've been doing for most of our lives. We have been storing up (hoarding) greed, fear, impatience, lust and hurt and then we wonder why everything we see and touch has been stolen and broken by the world and its devices (moth rust, thieves).

We wonder why we no longer see the value in our families and ourselves. The whole time God is patiently waiting for us to invest in something above ourselves (his kingdom) so we can overcome personal greed and fear. If you try to store your wealth, the moths will find it, or rust will consume it. If you try to hide it for yourself, thieves can steal it. Jesus is saying that earthly wealth/desires are very insecure. The things that we put before God rather it be wealth, job, people, or positions don't make us secure. Instead, Christ is showing us anything that we are investing in more than God, is the same thing that is causing us to be so insecure in our lives!

Do the majority of your investments (time & effort) go to being obedient to God and his kingdom or does it go to us and the wealth/desires of the world?

V21-

For where your treasure is, there your heart will be also. (NKJV)

The second test is the HEART TEST and God is asking us the humbling question, "Where is your heart really at?

Insert a commercial break----Where is treasure buried??

Since the beginning of time, man has always thought it was appropriate to bury our treasure in the ground. God says where our treasure is, there our heart is also. We have invested our heart into dirt of this world. Maybe this is why people say I feel like someone has literally trampled my heart. That is because we have put it in a position to be walked on, but God is showing us this is not the appropriate place.

Let's discuss MISPLACED hearts (heartache). The reason why some of us have the heartaches we have, is because of WHERE WE HAVE PLACED OUR HEARTS. When you place your heart into people first and not God this is the beginning of a dysfunctional relationship (when you TREASURE to please people/yourself more than God).

When we are placing our heart into people who have come from the ground and will return to the ground (Ecclesiastes 3:20) you are burying your heart in the ground (dirt). Where you plant yourself is how you see yourself, the way you see yourself is how you speak to others. Some of us are so unmindful of what we speak because we have misplaced our hearts in the people/world, so we treasure the world and not God.

Remember from the overflow of the mouth the heart speaks (Matthew 12:34).

The reason why some of us have a hard time seeing others/ ourselves let alone God, is because we are COVERED IN what we have planted ourselves in which is DIRT.

So, my QUESTION is this: How dirty do we have to get before we realize we are burying ourselves alive??

Back to our regularly scheduled program

What God is saying is that our heart follows our money.

That's not the way most of us think. We tend to think our money follows our heart. There is a saying that says,

"Whatever you invest your time in, is your God" and "whatever you spend your money on is important to you".

Too many of us spend all that we have on the things of this world and then we wonder why we have trouble concentrating on the things of God.

Our problem is that we've invested everything into people and the earth and hardly anything in heaven. Our money has kept our hearts tied to the earth.

We'll never be able to get our hearts focused on heaven as long as our heart is in material things. Possessions can very easily become the center of our life. If this continues to happen that means our possessions will own us and we will not own them.

V22-23

The third test is the MIND TEST and is found in verses 22-23: "The eye is the lamp of the body. If your eyes are good, your whole body will be full of light. But if your eyes are bad, your whole body will be full of darkness. If then the light within you is darkness, how great is that darkness!"

What Christ is showing us in this text, is the eye is a symbol for the mind. Jesus is saying that there are only two possible ways to look at things. If our minds focus only on things that are seen down here, we'll be full of darkness and disaster.

The natural eye focuses on our physical existence and the existence of materialism but the spiritual eye locks into what really matters (2 Corinthians 4:18). When money becomes our first priority, it can put blinders on our eyes and the heart of our spiritual life. If our hearts and thoughts are filled with how we can deposit treasures in heaven (meaning how can we please God), our bodies will be full of light.

V24

The fourth and final test is the MASTER TEST. This focuses on our will and asks the question: "Whom do you serve? Or whom will you serve?" Let's look at the text.

"No one can serve two masters. Either he will hate the one and love the other, or he will be devoted to the one and despise the other. You cannot serve both God and Mammon (money) NKJV."

To "serve" means that we've made a choice and engaged our wills. If we're not careful, we can be deluded by thinking material things will last forever. Our emotions can then affect our minds, which in turn can cause our wills to be in the grip of money with a capital "M."

The word Jesus uses here for money is the word, "Mammon," which is a proper noun, or a name for a demonic spirit. Jesus viewed Money as a rival for preeminence. Attachment to money leads to a demonic detachment from God. The Bible is absolutely clear about the unhealthy love of money.

To be a committed Christ-follower is not merely a matter of the emotions but also of our minds and wills. To love God requires service and even sacrifice. This type of allegiance cannot be rendered to two parties. Whatever we devote ourselves to becomes our God. The tension that many of us experience when we try to love both God and money will sooner or later begin to show where our real loyalty lies. Only one master will win out.

Money is not just a neutral medium of exchange, but a "power" with a life of its own which seeks to control, and even consume us. The goal of this Money Master (Mammon) is total domination of your value system, without you even being aware of it.

If you're serving the Money Master, Jesus says you will be unable to fully serve God. He doesn't say, "You better not" or "it would be unwise to serve both," He says, "You cannot serve both God and money." As such, how we handle our money has a lot to do with how serious we are about obeying God. His words are unsettling. If you love money, you will end up hating God. If you are devoted to the pursuit of possessions and the making of money, you will find yourself despising the things of God.

Hurt and Alone

———⚭———

Luke 8:26-33

"So, they arrived in the region of the Gerasenes, across the lake from Galilee. As Jesus was climbing out of the boat, a man who was possessed by demons came out to meet him. For a long time, he had been homeless and naked, living in the tombs outside the town. As soon as he saw Jesus, he shrieked and fell down in front of him. Then he screamed,

"Why are you interfering with me, Jesus, Son of the Most High God? Please, I beg you, don't torture me!" For Jesus had already commanded the evil spirit to come out of him. This spirit had often taken control of the man. Even when he was placed under guard and put in chains and shackles, he simply broke them and rushed out into the wilderness, completely under the demon's power. Jesus demanded, "What is your name?" "Legion," he replied, for he was filled with many demons. The demons kept begging Jesus not to send them into the bottomless pit. There happened to be a large herd of pigs feeding on the hillside nearby, and the demons begged him to let them enter into the pigs. So, Jesus gave them permission. Then the demons came out of the man and entered the pigs, and the entire herd plunged down the steep hillside into the lake and drowned." Luke 8:26-33 NLT

V 26-27 (impure spirit) God always shows up to break the cycle and interrupt the direction we were headed. What is a cycle? A cycle is a particular way of living that the people around you accept even though it embarrasses, degrades & exposes you. Some destructive cycles are masturbation, despair, fornication, adultery and idolatry. The enemy secludes us leaving us feeling abandoned, lost and without hope. V28-29 God's power always evicts what has been restricting us from seeing & following him. The device that is holding us is designed to keep us from acknowledging GOD. The voice that we speak, and people hear doesn't belong to us, it belongs to what is hurting us. The man didn't speak, the demon did.

What you submit to is what speaks for you. Whether it be peace or pain, whether it be Christ or your crisis. A strong hold's (demon's) job is to strip you, humiliate you and cause you to destroy yourself. A stronghold is *Self-Destructive.*

Why does the enemy want to strip us....to show our scars?

How does the enemy use our scars? The enemy uses our scars so we will attract more of what has attacked us. The man's scars were invisible to him but visible to everyone else. We don't even realize we have been marked by our past experiences until we make it into a new experience. V 30-31(Jesus asked, what is your name? Legion he replied) God did not seek to calm the man, but rather he confronted the demons that were abusing the man. Healing and deliverance come from Christ confronting our situation. Not from the world or people trying to calm us in our situation. 32-33 (pigs feeding on the hillside & demons were released inside the pigs. The pigs rush down into the steep bank of the lake). People who accept the cycle are a part of it, so they don't celebrate when God frees you from it. They were tolerating you for the sake of entertaining themselves. Demons are always eager to jump into what you hold as a profit so they can jump back into you. We have to stop getting attached to things, relationships, possessions that profit us but disgust God.

Helping Hand

—⟨∞⟩—

Genesis 2:18;
Ecclesiastes 4:9-10;
Mark 2:3-4

"Then the Lord God said, "It is not good for the man to be alone. I will make a helper who is just right for him." Genesis 2:18 NLT

"Two people are better off than one, for they can help each other succeed. If one person falls, the other can reach out and help. But someone who falls alone is in real trouble." Ecclesiastes 4:9-10 NLT

"Four men arrived carrying a paralyzed man on a mat. They couldn't bring him to Jesus because of the crowd, so they dug a hole through the roof above his head. Then they lowered the man on his mat, right down in front of Jesus." Mark 2:3-4 NLT

God instructs us through His Word that "…it's not good for man to be alone; I will make him a helper suitable for him" (Genesis 2:18). God was setting the pattern for family and mankind to move from ISOLATION to RELATION. From the very beginning God intended for us to have functional and meaningful relationships inside our family.

INVEST: "Two are better than one, because they have a good return for their labor": (Ecclesiastes 4:9 NIV) a. V9: The term good return means dividends paid on a wise INVESTment. In today's culture we seem to be more concerned with investing in careers, accumulating possessions and the approval of others. We may find ourselves hindered in our pursuit of God's peace for ourselves as well as time or energy to invest in our own family.

- This hindrance amounts to why our families are emotionally and mentally bankrupt.

- The best investment we make is not monetary. The best investments we make in our family is our time.

- The other investment we make is putting our heart into the WORD not the weather (Matt 14:28-29).

When we invest into the word and not the weather (feelings). It changes the PLACE (leave boat) in our life, the PACE (walking on water), our PERSPECTIVE (Peters ceiling had now become his floor) The reason there is no movement in our families is because we invested into how the weather/storm makes us feel and not into the direction the word is telling us to go. What we invest in is the direction we will go.

During moments of sitting or sinking PRAYER is our response. (Lord help me Matthew 14:30) So that during moments of sinking we don't lose ourselves in the storm. When someone is drowning, they don't make sounds they make signs. We have to do our best to be cognizant of our family and like Christ choose to elevate each other regardless of our failures.

BUILD: "If either of them falls down, one can help the other up. But pity anyone who falls and has no one to help them up." (Ecclesiastes 4:10 NIV) V10: Meaningful relationships BUILD us up; they lift us past our level of failures. (Failure is a result not a person).

Within each family, every person has problems but that doesn't make the person a problem. Acknowledging the problem and not defining the person by the problem says that we choose to attack problems not the person in order to bring peace. In order to initiate progress and growth, you have to feed the person's potential, not their problem. If we are going to know how to build the family, we must first know how the devil breaks it. In Genesis 3:6 we see the family was first broken by two things. Eve (by what she saw) and Adam (by what he heard). In order to build our family, we have to be mindful of what we put in their eyes and ears. When we cover these areas, our families will no longer have to hide behind our mistakes and hurts (fig leaves Gen 3:7)

CARE and CARRY US:

As a family, in order to CARRY each other we must first CARE for each other. The Bible says in Mark 2, there was a gentleman who was paralyzed and his four friends carried him on a rooftop (Mark 2:3-4) in order to get him closer to God so he could be healed. The friends took apart the roof of clay and dirt. In order to get our families and ourselves to a place we have never seen before with God we are going to have to dig through some dirt preferably our own.

Now let us imagine we are the man being carried.

He had to trust them with his hurt. iii. Let me show the vulnerability in our minds:

- "they might hurt me more if they drop me…"

- "they are going to see me in my brokenness (my mess)" iiii. This, however, is the truth about us:

- Everybody has a mat—let the mat stand as a picture of humanity, of our brokenness and imperfection.

- "It's what 's not 'normal' about me. It is the little 'not right' tag that I desire to hide.

- Sometimes we spend our whole lives doing 'mat management.'

  1. We pretend that we don't have a mat.

  2. We appear to be so healthy, so strong that our family and people around us assume that we can walk anywhere we want with

them and without them but truthfully, we can't.

REFLECTION: It is only when we allow our family to see our mat, we are able to give and receive help. A. God then shows us two things:

- How to trust while being vulnerable

- How to be faithful and dependable while helping those we love.

When this happens, the healing begins in our lives and our families. Meaningful relationships within our families and our lives HEAL us when we are too hurt to move.

Finding Strength

Judges 16:28-30

"Then Samson prayed to the Lord, "Sovereign Lord, remember me again. O God, please strengthen me just one more time. With one blow let me pay back the Philistines for the loss of my two eyes." Then Samson put his hands on the two center pillars that held up the temple. Pushing against them with both hands, he prayed, "Let me die with the Philistines." And the temple crashed down on the Philistine rulers and all the people. So, he killed more people when he died than he had during his entire lifetime." -Judges

The wrong mindset (Delilah) about love makes you feel like God has forgotten you. However, the right love comes from God alone when you choose to reconnect to it. Everything thatwas holding you back that you couldn't see is in a position to be moved by your doing and His power! Instead of asking God to remove you from the situation that you are stuck in, ask God to put you in the center of it so that your faith can tear down what's been tormenting you. There is only one way for God's strength to become permanent in your life. It is when you can no longer see your own and you are willing to die to the idea of it!! This is how the kingdom destroys cycles. From the inside out!! (Moses goes back into Egypt; Jesus comes in human form to take up a cross). Regarding the cycle that has been tormenting you, God is about to use you to break it.

Family Feud

Genesis 37:24-28

" Then they took him and cast him into a pit. And the pit was empty; there was no water in it. And they sat down to eat a meal. Then they lifted their eyes and looked, and there was a company of Ishmaelites, coming from Gilead with their camels, bearing spices, balm, and myrrh, on their way to carry them down to Egypt. So, Judah said to his brothers,

"What profit is there if we kill our brother and conceal his blood? Come and let us sell him to the Ishmaelites, and let not our hand be upon him, for he is our brother and our flesh." And his brothers listened. Then Midianite traders passed by; so, the brothers pulled Joseph up and lifted him out of the pit and sold him to the Ishmaelites for twenty

shekels of silver. And they took Joseph to Egypt."-
Genesis 37:24-28 NKJV

The activity of growth goes down before it
goes up. You will feel captive in a time that God has
called you to conquer.

You're not *stuck*, you're *stationed. One* scene
of your life is not the story of your life. Your story is
connected to the dream (purpose) inside of you. It's
not connected to the dirt around you (scene).

You are *under* what God called you to be
OVER. The dream will always contradict your
reality to see if we will focus on the mission of God,
or the place where people have left us.

If you focus on what's gone, you might lose
what you have left (yourself).

Be thankful for the gift of separation
(sanctification). Sanctification guarantees your
appetite and vision will never be on the same level
with the people who hurt you. (v25)

Just because someone helps you up, doesn't
mean they won't sell you out. A lot of people, family
included (these were his brothers) will help you out

of a mess, only to put you into something more dysfunctional. With God where you start is never where you stay. God uses our family's mistakes to take us to our destiny. Pain is NEVER the DESTINATION it is the TRANSPORTATION (v28) for purpose.

Watered Down Religion

———⊙⋈⊙———

Luke 2:41-49

"Every year Jesus' parents went to Jerusalem for the Passover festival. When Jesus was twelve years old, they attended the festival as usual. After the celebration was over, they started home to Nazareth, but Jesus stayed behind in Jerusalem. His parents didn't miss him at first, because they assumed, he was among the other travelers. But when he didn't show up that evening, they started looking for him among their relatives and friends. When they couldn't find him, they went back to Jerusalem to search for him there. Three days later they finally discovered him in the Temple, sitting among the religious teachers, listening to them and asking questions. All who heard him were amazed at his understanding and his answers. His parents didn't know what to think. "Son," his mother said to him, "why have you done this to us? Your father and I have been frantic, searching for you everywhere." "But why did you need to search?" he asked. "Didn't you know that I must be in my Father's house?"

Every year Jesus' parents went to Jerusalem for the Passover festival. When Jesus was twelve years old, they attended the festival as usual. After the celebration was over, they started home to Nazareth, but Jesus stayed behind in Jerusalem. His parents didn't miss him at first, because they assumed, he was among the other travelers. But when he didn't show up that evening, they started looking for him among their relatives and friends.

When they couldn't find him, they went back to Jerusalem to search for him there. Three days later they finally discovered him in the temple, sitting among the religious teachers, listening to them and asking questions. All who heard him were amazed at his understanding and his answers.

His parents didn't know what to think. "Son", his mother said to him, "why have you done this to us? Your father and I have been frantic, searching for you everywhere."

"But why did you need to search?" he asked. "Didn't you know that I must be in my Father's house?

Unfortunately, I have come to realize in today's culture, myself included, we tend to lose sight of Jesus (presence of God) based upon religious rituals and self-centered traditions. The Bible says it was not until after the religious festival was over that the master's parents realized that Jesus was no longer with them. They even assumed he was somewhere else with others and he was not. I learned a few things from this text. To this day, we still allow religious celebrations to keep us from seeing Jesus. We must also acknowledge that Jesus was not at their religious festivals. Meaning the presence of God was absent from their celebration. How many celebrations are we having, and Jesus is not even in attendance? When we lose sight of God, we begin to make assumptions about his movements that are inaccurate. Jesus' parents assumed where he was, and they were wrong; much like what we still do to this day. After three days they find Jesus in the temple asking questions and articulating scripture to the religious teachers. After asking Jesus questions, they received one of the most profound responses in scripture that I had overlooked. Jesus says, "Did you not know that I must be about my Father's business". From this particular piece of scripture, God showed me something that shook and shaped my worldview. He said son, you are taking me out of my business and by doing so, you have made it a privately owned business. (i.e. a prison) Meaning your faith, your work, your teaching, and your effort isn't freeing people the way God intended. It is holding them in place. You are not freeing the captives (Luke 4:18). You are helping to keep them in shackles. The Bible says, where the spirit of the Lord is, there is liberty, there is freedom (2 Cor 3:17).

Our faith through God's design frees others, if it doesn't then our faith is in our own agenda and not the spirit of God. Maybe this explains why most churches are filled with believers but not disciples; there is a difference. Maybe this explains why people go to church and exist but never are truly alive with purpose from God.

Or it could be why we have several churches in one community and the community is still collapsing. We seem to have a form of godliness but deny its power. Does that sound familiar?

If we study the patterns of Christ, we see that where and when there are assumptions, the religious rituals end and the Fathers' business begins. Once we realize something valuable is missing from our journey in life, we begin to seek Jesus and not our agendas. We are then led to a place of astonishment. In this place we see the authority of God (Jesus was twelve years old. Twelves equals authority) in a way that we never planned on.

Exhale

Psalm 40:1-2;
1 Kings 19: 2-15

I waited patiently for the Lord to help me, and he turned to me and heard my cry. He lifted me out of the pit of despair, out of the mud and the mire. He set my feet on solid ground and steadied me as I walked along. Psalm 40:1-2

"So Jezebel sent a messenger to Elijah to say, "May the gods deal with me, be it ever so severely, if by this time tomorrow I do not make your life like that of one of them." Elijah was afraid and ran for his life. When he came to Beersheba in

Judah, he left his servant there, while he himself went a day's journey into the wilderness. He came to a broom bush, sat down under it and prayed that he might die. "I have had enough, Lord," he said. "Take my life; I am no better than my ancestors." Then he lay down under the bush and fell asleep. All at once an angel touched him and said, "Get up and eat." He looked around, and there by his head was some bread baked over hot coals, and a jar of water. He ate and drank and then lay down again. The angel of the Lord came back a second time and touched him and said, "Get up and eat, for the journey is too much for you." So, he got up and ate and drank. Strengthened by that food, he traveled forty days and forty nights until he reached Horeb, the mountain of God. There he went into a cave and spent the night. And the word of the Lord came to him: "What are you doing here,

Elijah?" He replied, "I have been very zealous for the Lord God Almighty. The Israelites have rejected your covenant, torn down your altars, and put your prophets to death with the sword. I am the only one left, and now they are trying to kill me too." The Lord said, "Go out and stand on the mountain in the presence of the Lord, for the Lord is about to pass by." Then a great and powerful wind tore the mountains apart and shattered the rocks before the Lord, but the Lord was not in the wind. After the wind there was an earthquake, but the Lord was not in the earthquake. After the earthquake came a fire, but the Lord was not in the fire. And after the fire came a gentle whisper. When Elijah heard it, he pulled his cloak over his face and went out and stood at the mouth of the cave. Then a voice said to him, "What are you doing here, Elijah?" He replied, "I have been very zealous for the Lord God Almighty. The Israelites have rejected your covenant, torn down your altars, and put your prophets to death with the sword. I am the only one left, and now they are trying to kill me too." The Lord said to him, "Go back the way you came, and go to the Desert of Damascus. When you get there, anoint Hazael king over Aram." 1 Kings 19:2-15 NIV

Sometime ago, I had the privilege of helping my son with his science homework. Now let me help you envision something; my son is 6'3 which exceeds my vertical height. What I learned from my son's homework is how to use google and I learned a little bit about sinkholes. Studies show that most sinkholes occur when the underground resources gradually dry up, causing the surface to collapse from loss of support. From this, everything eventually caves forming a grotesque pit. What I've learned from living is that depression and sinkholes are parallel. Depression always seems to viciously overwhelm or should I say overshadow us. Depression is actually the result of an unhealthy process where inner resources are depleted. Until one day there is nothing left but emptiness and darkness. Unfortunately, depression is America's number one health problem. I believe it's a spiritually rooted (Isa 61:3 NKJV/NIV) problem that bears fruit in the physical, emotional and mental areas of our lives.

Studies have shown that half of all women struggle with depression and one out of every three men struggle with depression on a consistent basis. Regardless of ethnic backgrounds, social status or personal beliefs, depression is unbiased. The only way to consistently overcome it is with spiritual wisdom and emotional integrity.

That moment came for me in January 2003 when my father passed away. I was six years into a solid career in United States Air Force and I was stationed at Minot, ND. After he passed, I felt absolutely empty and completely exhausted. I had no idea how I had gotten to that particular point and what was more devastating was the fact I had no idea how to escape it. One day, I unexpectedly got a box from my mother with toys for my son and a Bible for me. In the front of the Bible one of the scriptures that my Mom had handwritten was

Psalm 40:1-2: "I waited patiently for the Lord; he turned to me and heard my cry. He lifted me out of the slimy pit, out of the mud and mire; he set my feet on a rock and gave me a firm place to stand". Honestly this was inception of my faith and from this, my journey defeating depression began. I believe the mire that is mentioned means the dirt or sediment at the bottom.

This past summer my daughter had me at the pool at least two or three times out of the week. She is the common denominator for fun in our house. One day while we were at the pool, I brought a beach ball to play with while in the water. My son and my daughter took turns throwing the ball and holding the ball under the water. They would hold the ball under the water until their arms got tired or until the ball would escape their grip, popping to the surface. I believe the mire in our life is like that beach ball. The sediment or hurt that we have never dealt with settles at the bottom of our hearts, at the bottom of our souls. It randomly pops up when we no longer have the energy to suppress it.

Unfortunately, this mire finds its way to the surface spilling ugliness and darkness into life. When this happens consciously and unconsciously, we choose to spread it by passing it to others who are around us. Mire comes in many different forms: hidden transgression, disappointment, fear, buried pain, rejection, or the loss of a loved one. The Bible shows us that Elijah wrestled with depression because he focused on the problem (Jezebel). On Mount Carmel, he   focused on the power and presence of God. After our greatest victories, we are often the most vulnerable to a fall. Elijah had just won an amazing victory for God, but suddenly he was so discouraged that he wanted to die. In his panic, he focused on the voice of his enemy rather than on the power of God to deliver him. From there on he had an emotional avalanche. Elijah was in the depths of anxiety when he said, "... I am no better than my fathers!" (1 Kings 19:4). There's an old saying that says, comparison is the thief of joy. Meaning comparing yourself to others will always rob you of your God given identity and peace of mind. Elijah's focus had shifted from the Lord to his circumstances (fears), and then from his circumstances to himself (self-doubt) than to his family history (past). You put all these things together and we find ourselves much like Elijah exhausted and overwhelmed.

The first thing he did to combat his depression was get some rest and refreshment. Then he acquired a new focus. Elijah believed that he was the only one in Israel who was spiritual and faithful. Elijah was in touch with his feelings, but he wasn't in touch with reality. Things weren't as bad as he thought, so God came to give Elijah a healthy dose of reality. What you pay attention to, you give access to you. Once God had Elijah's attention, He set out to readjust and access his thoughts. From this, he got new insight. When Elijah was down and had his back against the wall, the Lord told him to get up and get moving: "Go, return on your way to the Wilderness … and when you arrive, anoint Hazael as king over Syria" (1 Kings 19:15). God wanted him to make a choice of godly action based on obedience rather than inaction based on his emotions. Many people believe that life's pressures lead to depression. However, it's how we handle those pressures that lead us either to depression or to victory. I pray that if depression creeps in, you will follow God's remedy of rest, refreshment, refocus, new insight and obedient actions to God.

Resolving Conflict

Genesis 13:7-14

Have you heard the expression, "Time heals everything?" Unfortunately, that's not true. If time heals everything, you wouldn't ever need to see the doctor. Actually, time can make things worse. When you've got an open wound and you don't deal with it, it festers. From that anger turns to resentment, and resentment turns to bitterness.

The Bible says disputes broke out between the herdsmen of Abram and Lot. (At that time Canaanites and Perizzites were also living in the land.) Finally, Abram said to Lot, "Let's not allow this conflict to come between us or our herdsmen. After all, we are close relatives! The whole countryside is open to you. Take your choice of any section of the land you want, and we will separate. If you want the land to the left, then I'll take the land on the right. If you prefer the land on the right, then I'll go to the left." Lot took a long look at the fertile plains of the Jordan Valley in the direction of Zoar. The whole area was well watered everywhere, like the garden of the LORD or the beautiful land of Egypt. (This was before the LORD destroyed Sodom and Gomorrah.) Lot chose for himself the whole Jordan Valley to the east of them. He went there with his flocks and servants and parted company with his uncle Abram (Genesis 13:7-11). Here Abraham gave us an amazing example of how to handle conflict. He did not point fingers or try to win the dispute he set his heart on finding a solution. He did not try to make himself seem better or overly pious. He allowed Lot to choose first here we see resolving a conflict with someone else means putting them first and addressing what they want. I believe this is a disconnect in most of all our conflicts. We tend to put our wants first and neglect the other persons feelings. Doing this causes more harm than help. Abram invited Lot into his life. There are conflicts in our life that we invite, and those conflicts expose people and things that are interfering with our relationship with God.

The Bible says as soon as Lot left God begin to speak (Genesis 13:14). Abram could bring his wife (covenant relationship) but not his nephew. We cannot hear God or should I say God cannot speak into our lives when we invite things that He does not approve of (Genesis 12:1) it will create unnecessary conflict. Sometimes conflict shows us who or what we need to separate from in order to walk in our purpose from God.

Conscious Realignment

John 20:11-18

"But Mary stood outside by the tomb weeping, and as she wept, she stooped down and looked into the tomb. And she saw two angels in white sitting, one at the head and the other at the feet, where the body of Jesus had lain. Then they said to her, "Woman, why are you weeping?" She said to them, "Because they have taken away my Lord, and I do not know where they have laid Him." Now when she had said this, she turned around and saw Jesus standing there, and did not know that it was Jesus. Jesus said to her, "Woman, why are you weeping? Whom are you seeking?" She, supposing Him to be the gardener, said to Him, "Sir, if You have carried Him away, tell me where You have laid Him, and I will take Him away." Jesus said to her, "Mary!" She turned and said to Him, "Rabboni!" (which is to say, Teacher). Jesus said to her, "Do not cling to Me, for I have not yet ascended to My Father; but go to My brethren and say to them, 'I am ascending to My Father and your Father, and to My God and your God." Mary Magdalene came and told the disciples that *Conscious Realignment* she had seen the Lord, and that He had spoken these things to her."-John 20:11-18 NKJV

God speaks to the bent areas of your life. The areas where you were struggling. Your mind (Angel at the head) and direction of your life (Angel at the feet).

It matters who recognizes you, and no one can recognize you like God. Ask God to make you immovable to the words of people and culture but moveable (responsive) to His word (Acts 5:29). This isn't about being thick skinned. It's about asking the Creator for a new heart (Ezekiel 36:26).

When your faith isn't dictated by titles or people (the disciples had dispersed), sometimes God will reveal something to you in a place where others have run away (removed themselves). This is just so you hear and see God in a way that you hadn't before. Then you will realize you are on the outside of the vision that God is about to put inside of you, to redirect you and redirect others on where we should set our sight; Upward (ascension to God) not empty places that God use to be in (the tomb). The eternal God, the God of the Bible, is a God of movement. Purpose with Him isn't a parking lot and it isn't mundane. If we aren't moving towards the direction of destiny, then we are listening to everything except God.

Reassurance

Ruth 1: 16-18

B ut Ruth replied, "Don't urge me to leave you or to turn back from you. Where you go, I will go, and where you stay, I will stay. Your people will be my people and your God my God. 17 Where you die, I will die, and there I will be buried. May the Lord deal with me, be it ever so severely, if even death separates you and me." 18 When Naomi realized that Ruth was determined to go with her, she stopped urging her. Ruth reassured Naomi. You show love by reassuring someone they are not alone. Ruth wouldn't leave Naomi regardless of the circumstances. You show love by sticking with someone through tough times (LOVE has sticking power it always protects). Ruth told Naomi her people and her God were now hers. You show love by adjusting to others. Ruth said she wouldn't allow death to separate her. You show love by reaching beyond your comfort zone. (Reaching beyond our comfort zones causes for self-denial Luke 9:23) You show love by putting their needs above your needs.

Rerouting

1 Samuel 30:1-10

Three days later, when David and his men arrived home at their town of Ziklag, they found that the Amalekites had made a raid into the Negev and Ziklag; they had crushed Ziklag and burned it to the ground. 2 They had carried off the women and children and everyone else but without killing anyone.3 When David and his men saw the ruins and realized what had happened to their families, 4 they wept until they could weep no more. 5David's two wives, Ahinoam from Jezreel and Abigail, the widow of Nabal from Carmel, were among those captured. 6David was now in great danger because all his men were very bitter about losing their sons and daughters, and they began to talk of stoning him. But David found strength in the lord his God. 7Then he said to Abiathar the priest, "Bring me the ephod!" So

Abiathar brought it. 8Then David asked the lord, "Should

I chase after this band of raiders? Will I catch them?" And the lord told him, "Yes, go after them. You will surely recover everything that was taken from you!" 9 David and the six hundred men with him came to the Besor Valley, where some stayed behind. 10 Two hundred of them were too exhausted to cross the valley, but David and the other four hundred continued the pursuit. Purpose is activated by problems. What's missing in your life awakens it. When things in your life are being removed, it means you are being rerouted. It was David's decision to go to Ziklag not God's. The first place we see the residue of his decisions was at home (whether they are good or bad). The chaos in our life is connected to our choices in life. Ziklag reflects where you are at with God (David was running from his problems-Saul and his purpose (he was the next King). When you live in a state (Ziklag) that dishonors God, it will empty your life. How long was it before David talked to God? - 1 Samuel 23:4 (aka 7 chapters). When there is a disconnect in your relationship with God, it creates destructive detours in your family. Compromise with the world, offers only a temporary solution to our problems.

Proximity

1 Samuel 3:3-11;
Job 37:14

"The lamp of God had not yet gone out, and Samuel was sleeping in the Tabernacle near the Ark of God. Suddenly the Lord called out, "Samuel!" "Yes?" Samuel replied. "What is it?" He got up and ran to Eli. "Here I am. Did you call me?" "I didn't call you," Eli replied. "Go back to bed." So, he did. Then the Lord called out again, "Samuel!" Again, Samuel got up and went to Eli. "Here I am. Did you call me?" "I didn't call you, my son," Eli said. "Go back to bed." Samuel did not yet know the Lord because he had never had a message from the Lord before. So, the Lord called a third time, and once more Samuel got up and went to Eli. "Here I am. Did you call me?" Then Eli realized it was the Lord who was calling the boy.

So, he said to Samuel, "Go and lie down again, and if someone calls again, say, 'Speak, Lord, your servant is listening.'" So, Samuel went back to bed. And the Lord came and called as before, "Samuel! Samuel!" And Samuel replied, "Speak, your servant is listening." Then the

Lord said to Samuel, "I am about to do a shocking thing in Israel." 1 Samuel 3:3-11 NLT

"Pause a moment, Job and listen; consider the wonderful things God does" (Job 37:14 GNT).

I know this may sound simplistic but if you want to hear God's vision or get onboard with His plan, then you're going to have turn off a few things; starting with the television.

You can't listen to God and the TV at the same time! The Bible says "Pause a moment, Job and listen; consider the wonderful things God does" (Job 37:14 GNT).

You have to be quiet in order to hear God speak. The reason why we may never hear God speak to us is because we're never quiet. Something is always going on in our mind, so while God is trying to get through to us on the phone line of life, He's getting a busy signal. You've got to reserve time alone with God. My daughter is 7 going on 25. When she was little, she would wiggle all over the place. I believe as adults we struggle from spiritual wiggles, whether it be emotions, possessions, problems or careers. We cannot be still or quiet long enough to hear consistently from God. If we go a little bit further, scripture says, while Samuel was sleeping quiet and still, he heard God call his name. Before we go further, lets unpack this. Samuel was sleeping in the Tabernacle next to the Ark of Covenant (presence of God), while the lamp of God had not yet gone out. Samuel was being awaken in the dead of the night. God calls us while we are in darkness so the only light, we see will be Him.

Samuel heard God's voice. He was sleeping NEXT to God. In Other Words: Proximity is critical with God because it creates intimacy. When God calls you into consciousness, it takes you out of your place of comfort and out of your place of convenience. From consciousness we begin to pursue Gods word (voice). "The lamp of God had not yet gone out, and Samuel was sleeping in the Tabernacle near the Ark of

God. Suddenly the LORD called out, "Samuel!" "Yes?" Samuel replied. "What is it?" 1 Samuel

My mother and father would be in the dining room and my mom would be sharing something that she felt was important. However, my dad didn't like to just sit around and listen. He had to be doing something – straightening the furniture, straightening the desk etc. He would even drift into the kitchen and begin putting away dishes. Then it might occur to him that he needs to do something upstairs or in the living room (about 2-3 rooms away) … and my Mom's still talking. Rightfully so, she would get a little frustrated. Why does my Mom get frustrated you ask? Because she knew if

My Dad is not in the same room – He's probably not listening to her anymore. There can be no vision when there is division. If you're going to hear God's voice; if you're going to know His will – you have to be in the same room as Him.

"He got up and ran to Eli. "Here I am. Did you call me?" "I didn't call you," Eli replied. "Go back to bed." So, he did. Then the LORD called out again, "Samuel!" Again, Samuel got up and went to Eli.

"Here I am. Did you call me?" "I didn't call you, my son," Eli said. "Go back to bed." Samuel did not yet know the LORD because he had never had a message from the LORD before." When God calls you into consciousness, it takes you out of your place of comfort and out of your place of convenience. From consciousness we begin to pursue Gods word (voice).

God does this to impregnate us with a vision that comes from his voice alone. God calls the child, not Eli. He speaks to a surrendered life, not a selfish life.

The best part of Eli appears here — his understanding, his sympathy for Samuel. This is the use of all imperfect teachers and churches; not to demand our listening to them, but to send us to solitary converse and intimacy with God.

Time and Space

————◯✕◯————

Genesis 32:22-23

66T hat night Jacob got up and took his two wives, his two female servants and his eleven sons and crossed the ford of the Jabbok. After he had sent them across the stream, he sent over all his possessions." [2]

Create a space in time where everything you are familiar with (career, money, possessions and people) can no longer see you and you can longer see those things.

God is not going to allow us to be dependent on something that will deplete us.

A. What you walk into is determined by what you are willing to walk out of.

---

[2] *Jacob's two wives were Leah and Rachel (Genesis 29:23-28)*

B. What did he walk into... a place of surrender, a place of power, a place of being emptied (Jabokk)?

C. New beginnings are born from being emptied by God. What is God emptying you of? The rejection you have caused others and the frustration you feel from superficial (attractive on the outside empty on the inside) relationships. Leah equals rejection (Gen 29:31-32). Her name means tired cow (heifer). Imagine being unattractive and called a tired heifer. Jacob did not love Leah. He rejected her. All of us have faced some sort of rejection, like Leah. Because of this, we try to earn acceptance through actions/achievements. What people (Jacob) reject is what God selects. Gen 29:35 gives birth to Judah (fourth child). Jesus comes from this tribe. When God wants to bring Jesus to a generation, He always chooses the Leah's, the rejected ones. We are a chosen people, set apart to bring Jesus to the world.

D. Rachel equals frustration (Gen 30:1-2). Her name means ewe/sheep (mature female sheep). She was beautiful but she was empty. She was mature but counterproductive. It's possible to be like Rachel, outwardly looking like we've got it together, but inwardly hurting and miserable. Just because someone's life looks beautiful from the outside, doesn't mean it's fruitful on the inside. In today's culture we have figured out how to be liked by people, but we don't really like ourselves. From Rachel's frustration God gave birth to purpose, increase, and a dream (Genesis 30:22) (Rachel gives birth to Joseph). Where you were cannot touch where you are going. Where you are going with God will give birth to something new.

Misunderstood

———◯✕◯———

John 6:60-66

"Many of his disciples said, "This is very hard to understand. How can anyone accept it?" Jesus was aware that his disciples were complaining, so he said to them, "Does this offend you? Then what will you think if you see the Son of Man ascend to heaven again? The Spirit alone gives eternal life. Human effort accomplishes nothing. And the very words I have spoken to you are spirit and life. But some of you do not believe me." (For Jesus knew from the beginning which ones didn't believe, and he knew who would betray him.) Then he said, "That is why I said that people can't come to me unless the Father gives them to me." At this point many of his disciples turned away and deserted him."
John 6:60-66 NLT

Present insecurities come from past injuries. Jesus had done nothing wrong to anyone here.

Many people, I included, have allowed their offense to leave a relationship that empowered and elevated them. (A relationship that was needed.) Just because a feeling is real does not make it right.

A lot of us have turned away from God based on what we felt and what we misunderstood. In this case, the disciples thought Jesus was referring to cannibalism. As we know, he wasn't. He was seeing if they had a problem with digesting truth in their lives. They would not see elevation in their life, let alone movement from God. Human effort that is not centered and rooted by truth is in a state of paralysis. There is no forward movement when we move away from God. We have to be intentional on what we give our attention to, our feelings *or* our faith.

Drifting

Jonah 1:4-6

B ut the Lord hurled a powerful wind over the sea, causing a violent storm that threatened to break the ship apart. Fearing for their lives, the desperate sailors shouted to their gods for help and threw the cargo overboard to lighten the ship. But all this time Jonah was sound asleep down in the hold. So, the captain went down after him. "How can you sleep at a time like this?" He shouted. "Get up and Pray to your god!

Maybe he will pay attention to us and spare our lives."

There are different types of sleep found in scripture. One of the types of sleep I would like to discuss, is the sleep of *misdirection*. Sleep of misdirection is driven by emotions.

It's when we reject the word God has given us to accomplish his vision for humanity, based upon how we feel and what we think.

Somehow, we have *forfeited faith for feelings*. Jonah did not want to go to Nineveh because it was considered an unpopular nation. It's funny because that's still the problem today with the 21st century believer. We won't go to our God given assignments based upon how it looks and the fact that we don't care for the people. We care for the call though, just not the souls attached to it. How is it across America we have all these churches that are thriving, but the communities are collapsing? I don't exclude myself from the problem. I include myself because I'm guilty like everyone else. There are places I must go to for God that will make me uncomfortable, but in order to bring comfort to others I will have to step out of my comfort zone. Most of us were never taught when we neglect application of the word, that it disturbs everyone around us. In other words, sleep of misdirection disrupts our life and the lives of those around us. It causes others to make vain attempts to bring balance to a storm or situation they didn't cause.

Since we are asleep like Jonah, we are unaware of the storm and its effects on our environment. Some of the challenges and tragedies we see in our culture are because we have allowed pride, ethnic backgrounds, racism, and hate to disconnect us from God's plan of healing. A devotional I read by Hart Ramsey said something that shook me; "If your future looks dim because of your dark past, you're looking in the wrong direction. Start looking forward again". Much like Jonah, when we are headed in the wrong direction. We cannot point people to the right direction. Our job is to look forward to the Light.

One thing I have learned about facing light in my life is that it puts all the shadows and all the darkness behind you.

Bone Collector

Genesis 50:2

❝T hen Joseph made the sons of Israel swear an oath, and he said, "When God comes to help you and lead you back, you must take my bones with you." Genesis 50:25 NLT

Joseph fulfilled his purpose (dream) from God. Bones are a reminder (memory) of what was. God intends for us to "die with memories not with dreams", when you fulfill the call. The next generations will carry around tangible pieces of what God did through your faith. Too many generations of people have been left empty handed because many died with the dream. Pressure/ isolation (the pit) proves what we are advertising is real (Gen 37:5 & Gen 45:3-4). When you no longer surrender your allegiance to the patterns (cloaks: Gen 39:12-13 & Gen 37:23) of yesterday. You will begin to move forward. If you follow the patterns of hurt, you will remain hurt. What you follow is what you will find (Jer 29:13). The access point to JOY is not accumulation but appreciation to God.

The dream is connected to patterns of hope/healing/LOVE. The gift begins to grow and helps you outgrow your circumstances (the prison: Gen 39:19) It's not so much about what you see (the dream), it's what you cause others to see, (Gen 45:5) *Which is God!!*

Doors

2 Kings 4:4-5

T hen go into your house with your sons and shut the door behind you. Pour olive oil from your flask into the jars, setting each one aside when it is filled. So, she did as she was told. Her sons kept bringing jars to her, and she filled one after another.

The one thing I learned while establishing meaningful relationships is the greatest problem in life is not conflict, but it's complacency (lack of movement). One morning I was taking my son to school. We jumped into the car and I made an effort to put my car in drive and it would not start. After several minutes of frustration, my son pointed towards the dashboard because a light was on. The light read "door open" even though the doors appeared closed. So, we both began to get out of the car and look at the doors until I found the door that was open. Once I slammed that door shut, I got back into the car and when I put my car in drive, we began to move.

As soon as I put the car in drive, God said the reason there isn't any movement in many of the areas of your life son, is because there are still open doors. He said in order for there to be movement in your life, doors *have* to be closed.

Have you ever noticed when you are on an elevator and the doors are being held open, there can be no movement? But when the doors close you and everyone around you begin to move… The same principle is in effect with our lives and God. In 2 Kings 4:4-5, the widow was instructed by Elisha that after she got everything she needed (empty containers), he told her to close the door behind her and begin to work and live through the word God gave her. In order for there to be movement in our lives, we must close doors to the world, distractions, people and pain. When we begin to close doors, God begins to fill our emptiness inside of our homes, children, and ourselves. God will take what we overlooked and turn it into our overflow! But first we have to close some doors.

A Gift to Jamier

About Author

Carl Dixon is a visionary, cultural influencer and spiritual architect. He is an innovative leader that believes in investing into people. He's retired from the United States Air Force. He is currently pursuing his passion in sports medicine and fitness. His greatest accomplishment and joy are loving his wife and children and helping them enjoy a healthier and happier life.